IMAGES
of America

FORT DODGE
1850–1970

On the cover: Former president John F. Kennedy leads a campaign parade to draw the support of Fort Dodge. (Courtesy of the Webster County Historical Society; photograph by Ed Larson.)

IMAGES
of America

FORT DODGE
1850–1970

Roger B. Natte

ARCADIA
PUBLISHING

Published by Arcadia Publishing
Charleston, South Carolina

Library of Congress Catalog Card Number: 2008927314

For all general information contact Arcadia Publishing at:
Telephone 843-853-2070
Fax 843-853-0044
E-mail sales@arcadiapublishing.com
For customer service and orders:
Toll-Free 1-888-313-2665

Visit us on the Internet at www.arcadiapublishing.com

CONTENTS

ACKNOWLEDGMENTS

The purpose of this book is to provide a glimpse of the rich and varied history of the Fort Dodge community and acquaint the readers, especially the people of Fort Dodge, with a history of which many do not know.

All but a few of the photographs included come from the archives of the Webster County Historical Society that have been accumulated over the last 40 years. Thanks to the many people who have contributed, not just photographs, but all the records and papers that make up the society's collection, some of which were necessary to complete this book. Special acknowledgment should be made to the Bergeman Collection, over 12,000 negatives produced by local photographer Harold Bergeman, who recorded the life of the community from 1944 to 1968. It is a collection that has been barely touched for this work and offers great promise for future publications. Recognition should also be given to Pam Bygness and Bob Dunsmoor, who were willing to share their extensive and valuable postcard collections. I would be remiss in not acknowledging the work of Bob Halm, Gladys Meier, and Lois Craig, who weekly volunteer their time in helping organize the society's materials. In addition, Helen Smith cannot receive enough credit for the hours and hours of work that she has done in indexing the local newspapers, a task which I have already drawn upon and promises to reap great benefits for people who research local history in the future.

I would like to thank the Fort Dodge Public Library for graciously providing the room for the society's library and the Webster County Board of Supervisors for its annual allotment, which pays for all the archival and office supplies necessary for the preservation of our community's history.

Finally I appreciate all those people who patiently adjusted their interests and commitments to allow me the time and freedom to pursue this project.

INTRODUCTION

Fort Dodge was a community foreseen long before its actual establishment. In 1838, the War Department, in developing long-range plans for American western frontier defense, proposed a series of military posts stretching from Louisiana to the Canadian border. One of those proposed sites was on the upper Des Moines River near what would become the site of Fort Dodge. Even so, the post might never have materialized except for a series of minor incidents between the Native Americans and the newly arrived settlers, which led to a petition to Congress for increased frontier security in western Iowa.

In 1850, the post was established, first as Fort Clarke and later changed to Fort Dodge because of communications conflicts with a second Fort Clarke in Texas. The new post, meant to be temporary, consisted of just one company of some 80 soldiers and 22 buildings. After 30 uneventful months, the post was abandoned and sold to civilians.

The future of the little community was given a boost when the federal land office was located there in 1855. The next year, largely due to a western land boom, prices soared from $1.25 an acre to $12, and the population of the community rose to over 1,000, mostly speculators seeking a quick buck but not a permanent home. Nevertheless, land profits served to fuel future investments in Fort Dodge.

The new community was blessed with natural resources such as coal, limestone, clay, and gypsum. It was coal that attracted railroads needed to insure general economic growth, but it was gypsum that put Fort Dodge on the map. By 1900, Fort Dodge was producing 25 percent of the world's supply of plaster, and the county was Iowa's leading producer of clay products.

By 1900, Fort Dodge was blessed with enlightened community leadership. Influenced by the great World's Columbian Exposition of 1893 in Chicago, dreams were for a city exceeding 50,000 by 1950. Nationally recognized architects were hired to design the buildings worthy of those dreams. By 1920, Fort Dodge was able to boast of more skyscrapers per capita than any other city in the Midwest, if not the nation.

The city was the political center of the state. No other could claim three U.S. congressmen, two U.S. senators, the director of the U.S. Mint, the solicitor of the Department of the Treasury, a third-party candidate for vice president, and a leading muckraking journalist who would become advisor for three presidents.

People of significance who have had Fort Dodge as their home include Karl L. King, leading composers of marches; William S. Kenyon, U.S. senator and circuit court of appeals judge; Jonathon Dolliver, U.S. senator; Libbie Hyman, internationally recognized zoologist; Lorenzo

Coffin, leader in agrarian reform and railroad safety legislation; Samuel Arkoff, Hollywood film producer; and Corita Kent, popular artist of the 1960s, among many others.

Fort Dodge did not achieve the dreams of growth of the earlier generation. Its economy today is essentially based upon being a retail and service center for north-central Iowa.

One

HUMBLE BEGINNINGS

The first white people to permanently stay in the Fort Dodge area were John Lott and his family, who first settled near the junction of the Des Moines and the Boone Rivers. Their presence led to tensions between the settlers and the remaining Native Americans. One incident, the death of Mrs. Henry Lott, an indirect result of Native Americans depredations in 1848, led to the settlers' demand that the federal government act to provide greater frontier protection.

In 1850, a company of the United States 6th Infantry was ordered to establish a post near the forks of the upper Des Moines River to police western Iowa. The troops remained for a relatively uneventful 30 months. The post's sutler or merchant, William Williams, left the sketch above of the post. It consisted of 22 log buildings with no stockade and was located just north of what is now the city square.

Officers were West Point graduates, most of exceptional ability. Most were from the South, and with the outbreak of the Civil War, all but one joined the Confederate army. Commanding officer Samuel Woods rose to the rank of colonel, stayed with the Union, and was paymaster general for the army west of the Mississippi River. The most notable was Louis Armistead (pictured here), who achieved fame when he died leading Picket's Charge at Gettysburg.

The post was abandoned in April 1853, and the site was purchased by the post sutler William Williams. Considered the founder of Fort Dodge, he platted the town and was to become its first mayor. Williams also led a rescue expedition to Spirit Lake, the scene of a massacre that killed more than 30 settlers.

After the troops left, only a handful of people remained until 1855 when the federal land office was established here. All federal land sales were made through Fort Dodge. The next two years, land sales boomed, prices soared to as much as $12 an acre, and the population reached 1,000. One of the earliest buildings was the Wahkonsa Hotel, which provided the best accommodations in town.

In 1857, with the collapse of the land boom, the town returned to a sleepy little frontier town. This photograph was taken looking north on Fifth Street from the city square. The buildings in the background are buildings from the military post. Unpaved and muddy streets were common in most Iowa towns, and cattle were allowed to roam freely in Fort Dodge until the 1880s.

This building, located at First Avenue North and Fifth Street, was the first brick building constructed after the post was abandoned. It served as the post office, doctor's office, courthouse, and drugstore. The section on the right was added later. The photograph dates to about 1912.

The structure was finally razed about 1963, but part of its foundation still remains as the north wall of a low-level storage building. Other than a log cabin, which has been moved and is now part of the Fort Museum, this is the last structure dating to the original settlement.

The original county seat was located at Homer about 16 miles south and east of Fort Dodge. In 1857, after a bitter fight, voters approved the move of the center of government to Fort Dodge, and this courthouse was constructed at the site of the current courthouse. Originally it was planned that the building would have a cupola; however, lack of funds forced the postponement of that addition until 1885.

Although many of the land speculators moved on after the 1857 land bust, some with hopes for the future invested in businesses and buildings. Shown here is the north side of the square from Sixth Street about 1870. Note the prominence of the billiard hall.

One of the most successful of the early merchants was James Swain, who built this commercial building, at Seventh Street and Central Avenue, and the Vincent House, now on the National Register of Historic Places. His wife was a true Renaissance woman. Adeline Morrison Swain was a scientist, a leader in women's rights, an advocate for farmers' interests, an educational reformer, and the first woman in Iowa to run for a statewide office. She is a member of the Iowa Women's Hall of Fame.

Further changes came rapidly. Several years later, Swain's building was incorporated into a larger commercial block. The adjacent building held the newspaper and printing firm owned by Benjamin Gue, who later served as the lieutenant governor of Iowa.

In 1856, at the height of the land boom, five churches were organized. There are no known photographs of any of the church structures other than the Presbyterian church shown here. It served the congregation from 1858 until it was replaced in 1891.

One of the finest residences in the community was Fair Oaks, home of John F. Duncombe, one of the city's first attorneys and an active land speculator. Arriving in Fort Dodge in 1854 with very little capital, he acquired a large enough fortune to be able to build this home in 1862. It was located where Fair Oaks Middle School is today and was razed in 1930. Duncombe later invested in railroads, in coal mining, and in the gypsum industry and served in the Iowa legislature and on the Iowa Board of Regents.

Fair Oaks was constructed of gypsum, a soft stone subject to weathering and deterioration. Another early home constructed of gypsum was the one shown here. The last such building in the city, it was located at the east end of the Herring Viaduct and was demolished about 1961.

Immediately after the Civil War, the Des Moines River was dammed to provide power for Hinton's flour mill. It was better known as Arnold's Mill, after its second owner. Prior to its establishment, the closest source of flour was 65 miles downriver. The width of the river made it difficult to maintain the dam, and it washed several times. The last time was in 1880, and the mill burned shortly after.

The turning point in the history of Fort Dodge was the coming of the railroad in 1869. R. D. T. Travis, an itinerant artist, has left this lithograph of the town of that time. From left to right on the skyline, the building with the tower is Lincoln School and close to it is the courthouse. The cupola is yet to be added. The two-story building on the far right is Fair Oaks, John F. Duncombe's home. In the center of the picture are a brickyard and the railroad depot.

With the arrival of the railroad in 1869, Duncombe built what was considered to be the finest hotel in northern Iowa. It was located on the west side of the square and lasted until it burned in the late 1980s. It remained the hotel of choice until 1910.

Lincoln School was the second building constructed as a school in the city and was located where the Phillips Middle School athletic field is today. The high school occupied the third floor. The building was completed about 1870, and the first class to graduate from high school was in 1876. By the 1950s, the building had deteriorated to the extent that it had to be abandoned and razed.

Two

GROWTH AND GLORY

The growth of Fort Dodge was slow until the arrival of the railroads in 1869, but in the next 30 years, the population quadrupled, and the economy diversified and expanded. Farsighted leadership invested in the community with an optimistic belief in the town's future. Some of the Midwest's finest architects were employed to design buildings that would provide for years of rapid growth. Community leaders, influenced by the great World's Columbian Exposition of 1893 in Chicago, adopted the latest technology and the ideas of the City Beautiful movement and progressive reform.

In 1903, Adolph Dittmer, a local amateur photographer, took a series of photographs documenting Fort Dodge at the beginning of the new age when many of the earliest buildings downtown were being replaced. The photograph above was taken from West Fort Dodge. Identifiable buildings on the skyline are, from left to right, Wahkonsa School, Tobin College, the courthouse, Corpus Christi Church, Lincoln School, the high school, the Methodist church, the Presbyterian church, and the first city water tower.

Many of the Dittmer photographs were taken from the clock tower of the new courthouse. This photograph was taken looking west down Central Avenue toward the city square. On the near side of the city square with the tower is the Garmoe Building, which still stands. Just beyond the city square is the Duncombe Hotel, and beyond it is the Heath Flour Mill. On the left in the distance is the Green and Wheeler Shoe Company. Note the existence of smoke hovering over the city, the result of the use of local low-grade coal for fuel.

Looking east from the courthouse, the Oleson Drug Company is in the foreground, then the post office with its twin towers, and, on the top left, the first building constructed solely for a high school.

City Park, Ft. Dodge, Ia.

The city square was the first park and was dedicated for public use when the town was first platted. It had served as the parade ground for the military post and as a place where farmers could leave their horses while doing business. The city square was redesigned several times over the years to make it parklike. This postcard, dated 1910, shows the streetcar line running through the city square, the Duncombe Hotel built in 1869, and the first bandstand.

Central Avenue looking east had taken on this appearance in 1905. The "Big Store" was the McQuilkin Furniture Store, a fixture downtown until after World War II. The building still stands today adjacent to the Boston Center. In the center at the far end is the Chicago Great Western Railroad depot.

Also in 1905, looking west from Eleventh Street, the streetcar tracks and the street paving can be seen. In the early 1890s, the streets were paved with bricks produced locally. After 1900, the bricks were replaced with wooden blocks to cut the sound of horses' hooves and make for a quieter downtown. Notice that the buildings were still wood frame, a construction that would soon be forbidden for downtown commercial buildings as a fire hazard.

The automobile had clearly come to Fort Dodge as seen in this photograph of Central Avenue from Tenth Street about 1925. The Wahkonsa Hotel is on the left.

The first 15 years of the 20th century can well be seen as Fort Dodge's golden age. It might be dated from the construction of the Beaux-Arts-style courthouse, still the most identifiable and imposing building in the city. Constructed in 1902, it set the tone for construction for the next 15 years. One of the Midwest's leading architects, Henry C. Koch of Milwaukee, was selected with the instructions to design a building "worthy of a city poised on the verge of greatness."

Koch also was chosen to design the local Carnegie library. In contrast to the Beaux-Arts courthouse, the Carnegie library is in classical Greco-Roman style. As shown in this photograph, it initially was a single-story structure, but a second story was added in 1932. The building housed the public library for 90 years before it moved to its new home on the city square. Both the courthouse and the library are on the National Register of Historic Places.

The First National Bank building, at 629 Central Avenue, was constructed in 1908 and was seen as an enormous undertaking for the time. By the definition of the time, a building of five stories or more was considered to be a skyscraper. By 1925, nine buildings of five or more stories had been completed downtown, allowing Fort Dodge to boast of more skyscrapers per capita than any city in the Midwest. The building is on the National Register of Historic Places.

Not only did Fort Dodgers have faith in the city's future, but outsiders also saw the promise. Richard Snell, an Illinois investor, constructed the seven-story Snell Building, at 805 Central Avenue, in the Chicago commercial building style and designed by the leading Iowa architectural firm of Liebbe, Rasmussen, and Nourse. The proximity to the courthouse made it a favorite location for lawyers' offices. Two more commercial-style buildings, the Boston Store and the McNamara Building, were adjacent to the east.

Prusia Hardware Company, at 608 Central Avenue, soon laid claim to be Fort Dodge's tallest at eight stories. Besides being a retail store, the company was also a large wholesale house serving five states. The city's excellent rail connections made Fort Dodge a leading wholesale trade center for many products. By 1915, the city laid claim to being home for over 500 traveling salesmen.

Prusia Hardware was built about 1915. Note the construction methods being used.

The Oleson Drug building was located at 802 Central Avenue and was completed in 1894 by O. M. Oleson, the city's leading entrepreneur and philanthropist. The building is noteworthy for its blend of architectural styles and elements. Although appearing to be two separate buildings, it, in reality, was built as a single structure. The building was demolished in 1971, and the site is now a parking lot.

The first building erected as a post office and federal building was completed in 1886 at 902 Central Avenue. Its distinctive twin towers made it one of the most identifiable structures in the city.

By 1908, the post office had become too small to meet the local needs. Its replacement, constructed at the same site, is a good example of America's rapidly changing architectural tastes. This second building was razed in 1962, and the site is now the Trolley Center.

The Carver Building, at 1003 Central Avenue, started as a two-story commercial building of little architectural significance that replaced the Italianate-style Carver residence and clinic at the time of World War I. The rapid development of downtown caused the owners to add another six floors for offices in 1922. Its occupants were primarily doctors and health professionals.

The Physicians Office Building at the corner of First Avenue North and Tenth Avenue was also a building whose upper stories were a later add-on, as can easily be seen in this photograph. As the name indicates, it was built originally for doctors' offices, but because downtown living was desirable, an additional four floors were added for apartments.

The Fort Dodge YMCA was organized in 1890 to offer educational and recreational opportunities to young men. This handsome structure at 604 First Avenue North, completed in 1910, was to be its home for 60 years. When built it included the latest in recreational facilities plus rooms for single men. Its swimming pool was the first in the city. It was demolished about 1963, and the site is now the Frontier Telephone Company building.

Although blessed with an abundance of new commercial buildings, Fort Dodge was sadly lacking in good hotels. In 1910, the problem was remedied with the completion of the Wahkonsa Hotel, considered to be one of the most grand in northern Iowa. It provided everything: a fine restaurant, a barbershop, a beauty shop, a shoe shine parlor, a men's clothing store, and a tobacco shop. The Wahkonsa Hotel was just one reason why Fort Dodge was seen as a honeymoon destination city in the second decade of the 20th century.

The Cadwell Building, on Eleventh Street and Central Avenue, was another apartment building. For most of its history, the front ground level was a news and tobacco store and the passenger station for the electric interurban railroad, which was on the Eleventh Street side. Note the water tower in the background. Constructed around 1890 by the Chicago Iron Company, its design with a hemispheric bottom received national attention as a great technological advance.

Fine architecture was not limited to office buildings, public buildings, and apartments but carried over to warehouses as well. The Leighton Electrical and Plumbing Wholesale Company erected this building before World War I. It is one of the few buildings that has not seen a change in its function. The building included inventory showrooms and what the company advertised as a restaurant and an elegant meeting and banquet room.

Three

Horses and Trains, Autos and Planes

The first 20 years of the existence of Fort Dodge was a period of relative stagnation and lack of growth. One of the major reasons was the lack of transportation. Certainly few things changed over the years as much as the nature of transportation. The soldiers walked to reach Fort Dodge, and their supplies were carried by wagon. In the 1850s, there was an attempt to make the river navigable and bring in steamboats. Success only came with the arrival of the railroads in 1869. Fort Dodge was to be served by four railroads giving direct connections with Omaha, Sioux City, Sioux Falls, Minneapolis, Des Moines, and Chicago. In 1915, 35 passenger trains served the city every day. The railroads were the city's leading employers. Railroads dominated until the 1920s, when automobiles made inroads into passenger travel and the public began to demand better roads. In the 1950s, the movement was toward air travel.

Fort Dodge was a walking town until 1910. Most people did not own a horse but could always rent one from one of the liveries. In 1908, the town could claim 10 liveries. The largest was Colby Brothers on the north side of the city square. The site was chosen because of its proximity to the railroad station, most of the hotels, and the nearby businesses.

Deliveries were all made by horse and wagon, as seen with the legendary Wells Fargo wagon. In 1912, the Wells Fargo office was located at 11 South Ninth Street.

The Des Moines River and the creeks that ran into it posed major obstacles to travel. Before the Civil War, two ferries provided the answer, the Colburn Ferry near what is now Kenyon Road and the McCaulley or Bob's Ferry above the mouth of the Lizard Creek. Shown here is what is believed to be the first bridge in Fort Dodge. It was built after the Civil War and located at the south end of Third Street. It was replaced in the 1880s by a double-span iron bridge.

Bennett Viaduct, completed in 1910, replaced the 1880s iron bridge. Faced not only with the need for a new bridge across the river but also a better and safer way to cross the railroad yards, it was decided to build one bridge crossing the area called the Flats as well as the river. It was unique in that it had a third entry ramp, by which the bridge could be entered from below and was built strong enough to carry a proposed streetcar line.

The first railroad to reach Fort Dodge was the Iowa Falls and Sioux City, a subsidiary of the Illinois Central Railroad, which was completed in August 1869. Shown here in this 1905 photograph is the passenger depot at Fourth Street and Fourth Avenue South, which served both the Minneapolis and St. Louis Railway and the Illinois Central Railroad.

2112. I. C. R. R. Passenger Station, Fort Dodge, Ia.

This Illinois Central Railroad depot was built in 1911. At its peak about 1915, the depot served 25 passenger trains a day. Two trains each way daily provided direct connections with Chicago on the Illinois Central Railroad line. One could leave Fort Dodge at 11:00 p.m. and be in Chicago by 7:00 a.m., getting a good night's sleep in the Pullman. Passenger service was discontinued in 1968, and the depot was razed in the 1990s.

Just to the east of the Illinois Central Railroad passenger depot was the freight depot. Both depot buildings were listed on the National Register of Historic Places prior to their demolition.

The photograph above is of the Illinois Central Railroad yards about 1947. Shown here are the roundhouse and the water tower. Steam locomotives were used until the early 1950s, when they were replaced by diesel. The roundhouse was abandoned and razed in 1989.

The Minneapolis and St. Louis Railway had its yards in the Pleasant Valley area at Eleventh Avenue Southwest and Tenth Street, almost under the Chicago Great Western bridge. Before 1901, the passenger station was located there too. The freight depot still stands at 134 Central Avenue, the only structure that still stands dating back to the railroad's days of glory.

The Chicago Great Western Railroad, previously the Mason City and Fort Dodge, built into Fort Dodge about 1886 and provided passenger connections with Minneapolis, Omaha, and Des Moines until 1965. The railroad's yards extended along Central Avenue east from Twelfth Street with the passenger depot, completed in 1905, facing Twelfth Street. The structure was demolished in 1963, and the yards were moved to east Fort Dodge.

One of the signature structures in Fort Dodge is the Chicago Great Western Railroad bridge crossing the Des Moines River. Fifty-two feet short of a half mile long and 140 feet high, it is the second-largest bridge in Iowa and was completed in 1903 after 18 months of work.

Originally a steam line, the Chicago Great Western Railroad added gas-electric units, such as in 1912, to provide short-run passenger service into Fort Dodge and down to Lehigh. Later the Minneapolis and St. Louis Railway also used gas-electric units.

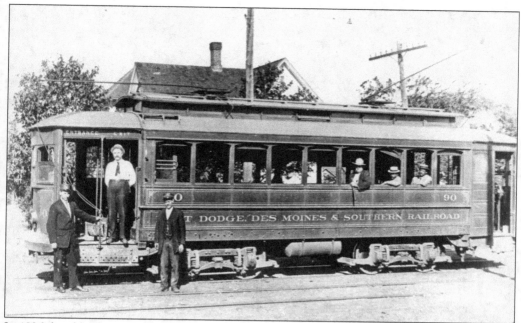

In 1896, local businessmen began construction of an electric streetcar line, primarily to connect the three railroad passenger depots. In 1901, it was extended to southeast Fort Dodge in the Oleson Park area as a way to encourage the residential development of that area. In 1905, the line carried a one-day record of 583 passengers.

In 1907, the streetcar line was purchased by the Fort Dodge, Des Moines and Southern Railroad, and it was integrated into an all-electric interurban service between Fort Dodge and the capital city. The passenger station was located at Hine's Drug Store, 712 Central Avenue. Passenger cars left Fort Dodge every two hours, starting at 5:00 a.m. and returning at 11:00 p.m. Some of the runs included both a passenger and a parlor car. The depot was located at First Avenue South and Fifteenth Street.

Streetcar service through town was discontinued in 1926, a victim of competition with the automobile. The passenger station was relocated to Eleventh Street and then to First Avenue South and Fifteenth Street, the current location of the YMCA. The Fort Dodge line continued the electric interurban service until 1954, when a flood destroyed its power-generating station. It then switched to all-diesel power.

The first automobile in Fort Dodge was a Winton purchased in 1899 by a clothing store owner, L. E. Armstrong. A real novelty, it was purchased more as a toy than a means of transportation, and Armstrong offered anyone who purchased a suit of clothes a ride around the city square. The *Fort Dodge Messenger* referred to the Winton as Armstrong's "Ought to Go" cart. By 1901, 25 automobiles were registered in the city.

In 1912, the Colby Brothers Livery Stables, the largest in the city, was sold to Jerry Coughlin, who changed it into an automobile livery, a symbolic beginning of the end of the horse era.

Here is an automobile on Seventh Street facing Central Avenue. Often people in the early years used the cars only in the warmer months, putting them in storage from December through February.

Shown here are the widow and son of Sen. Jonathon Dolliver in about 1912. Neither she nor her late husband ever drove, but like many other well-to-do people, she depended upon a chauffeur.

Early mechanics learned by looking and doing at a local garage, sometimes building their own vehicles from bottom up. Notice the suits and white shirts. In 1903, a man named de Loura opened a shop in a foundry at Central Avenue and Twenty-second Street to manufacture vehicles. Three cars, two runabouts and one touring car, were built before it folded.

Eight years after the Wright brothers completed their first heavier-than-air flight in December 1903, J. C. Turpin, a representative of the Wright aircraft company, executed the first flight in Fort Dodge in August 1911. Within a month of his Fort Dodge flight, Turpin set a world altitude record of over 9,000 feet.

Returning World War I veterans exhibited an interest in aviation, and in 1919, a field was established near what is now East Lawn Cemetery and sold the next year to automobile dealer and aviation enthusiast W. B. Swaney. The field was 60 acres and included a hangar and seven planes. This photograph is of one of the early pilot training classes. Swaney's venture failed, and the field was abandoned in 1925.

Charles Lindbergh's transatlantic flight renewed interest in flying in Fort Dodge. In 1928, the Fort Dodge Junior Chamber of Commerce reopened the airfield. Four years later, Ray Eno purchased 200 acres on the south side of the highway, built two large hangars, and dedicated Eno Airport on July 30, 1933. Many Fort Dodgers got their pilot's training under Eno.

This is dedication day for the current municipal airport, opened north of the city in 1952. The new airport was largely due to the efforts of Ed Breen, owner of the local radio station who was concerned with the need to insure commercial airline service to the city. Democratic presidential nominee Adlai Stevenson spoke at the dedication ceremonies.

Four

MINING AND MANUFACTURING

In its early years, Fort Dodge fortunes were made through land speculation, but realistically the economy depended upon agriculture. By the 1870s, mining increasingly became important, and as late as the 1930s, the city claimed the title of "Iowa's Mineral City." The Fort Dodge area has been blessed with bountiful mineral resources, such as coal, gypsum, limestone, clay, and gravel. In addition, the deep river valley made access to these resources easy. Coal was the first mineral mined. It was the coal that attracted the railroads, and the railroads in turn encouraged other industries. By the 1890s, industry and manufacturing had become increasingly important, and the economic base became increasingly diversified.

Coal mining began with the soldiers at the military post. Many of the mines were small operations such as this one, dug into the hillside and selling its product on the local market. Larger operations, employing as many as 100 miners, came later and shipped their product by railroad. Mining continued in the area until 1946 when the last mine closed.

Fort Dodge has always been most famous for its gypsum. The industry got its start about 1872 when the first mill was established to produce stucco. The earliest gypsum mining was by quarry, working the rock that was near the surface. Mules and horses provided the power for hauling.

It was not until 1895 that shaft mines were used. The last shaft mining ended about 1950 with a return to quarrying.

The Plymouth Gypsum Mill, shown here, was opened in 1904. By then most of the gypsum production was going into plaster for walls, something that was invented in Fort Dodge by George Ringland in 1884. Over the years, there were 29 different gypsum companies around Fort Dodge, and in 1900, five plants were operating.

The clay products industry got much of its impetus from the rapid growth of the towns around the dawn of the 20th century. One of the largest plants was the Vincent Clay Products plant south of Fort Dodge. This photograph dates from the 1920s.

Much of the land in north-central Iowa was wetland and only tillable if it could be drained. From the 1890s until 1920, floating barges, such as the one shown here, were used to dig drainage ditches.

Clay tile was needed to complete the drainage system. The Superior Clay Works shown here was located on Ninth Street on Soldier Creek in the 1920s near Snell and Crawford Parks. Other significant plants in Fort Dodge were located near the Hawkeye Avenue bridge, in southeast Fort Dodge, and in West Fort Dodge.

An often overlooked resource of the area is limestone. It was used infrequently in early years, except as building foundations, and it was not until the 1920s, when Iowa began surfacing its roads, that limestone mining became a viable business. Welp and McCarten opened a mine using mules for hauling in the late 1920s, just west of what is now Highway 169.

The steam-powered Imperial, or Blanden, Mill went into operation in 1882. Note the smoke from the chimney and the railroad car at the lower right. Its location is uncertain, although it was on the railroad along the river. Three or four local mills operated at the same time before 1900.

By far the most important of the Fort Dodge mills was the Heath Mill, located at the west end of Central Avenue. Opened about 1892, it claimed to be the largest oatmeal mill in the world, producing 4,000 barrels of flour or oatmeal a week and having world markets. Later it was owned by Quaker Oats. In 1940, it began to process soybeans, a product that was just being introduced to Iowa farmers. In 1943, it was acquired by Cargill. The plant ceased production in 1982 and was dismantled in 2005.

The Heath Mill, also known as the Great Western Cereal Company, producer of Mother's Oats, was a major employer of young women, who were hired to package the products for the retail trade.

The west end of Central Avenue was the primary industrial area for Fort Dodge. This aerial view shows, from the top down, the Tobin Packing Company plant, the city water plant, Standard Oil Company, Quaker Oats Mill, and Loomis Produce. The city reservoir, which still exists although no longer used, can be seen on Duck Island.

Fort Dodge has had several slaughterhouses in the 19th and early 20th centuries, but the first modern one was the Tobin Packing Company plant, a hog processor that opened in Fort Dodge in 1934, bringing jobs and a welcome relief to the local economy suffering from the depths of the Depression. In 1936, it processed 3,000 head of hogs and shipped 50 carloads of meat each day.

In 1954, the plant was acquired by George A. Hormel and Company, which continued to operate the plant until the 1980s. It was the city's largest and highest-paying employer.

The Iowa Beef Processors plant, located southwest of the city, also opened in the 1950s, but it closed in the 1970s after suffering labor problems.

At the beginning of the 20th century, the Green and Wheeler Shoe Company, located at 300 First Avenue South, produced high-quality women's and children's shoes. The company was acquired by a national firm in St. Louis, and the building was sold to the Monarch Telephone Company. In the 1930s, the building was acquired by the Fort Dodge Serum Company.

The Fort Dodge Serum Company was organized in the early part of the century to develop and produce a serum to prevent hog cholera. It became one of the mainstays of the Fort Dodge economy and one of the world's largest producers of animal pharmaceuticals.

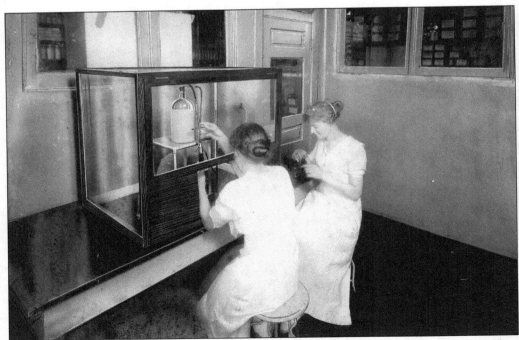

The laboratories and shipping departments were located in the old Green and Wheeler Shoe Company. In the 1950s, the company moved all its operations northwest of town.

The original plant of the Mulroney Manufacturing Company, a manufacturer of the Fort brand of men's work clothes, was located at 921 Central Avenue in a building that previously had housed the Fort Dodge Grocery Company. Around 1910, the company built its own plant at 702 First Avenue North.

This photograph of the Mulroney Manufacturing clothing shop in its original location offers some interesting insights into a workplace of the times. It was unusual to have men and women working together at similar tasks. Notice also that the shop appears to be clean and well lit. Finally note that the men are wearing white shirts. In the 1920s, the company was sold to Marso Rodenborn, which produced work and recreational gloves.

The Koll Brewery was built on the side of Soldier Creek shortly after the Civil War. Caves were dug into the hill side for storage. There were also two other breweries and one distillery in the late 1800s. The coming of prohibition in 1883 closed them down. This building was razed in 1916.

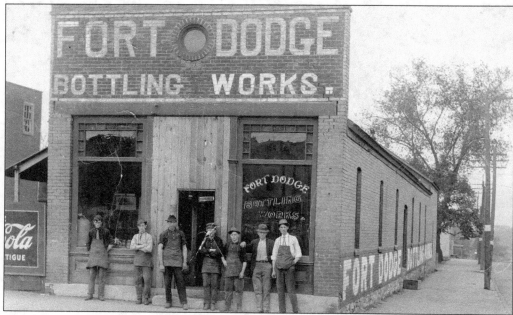

The Fort Dodge Bottling Works dates back to the 1870s. It was founded by a man name Noe, who promoted the business as the producer of "temperance drinks" and cider. The company was eventually sold to Henry Gill, who continued to operate the business until World War II. Gill developed a soft drink called Pale Moon, which had a national market in the 1930s.

A. R. Loomis first established an egg and poultry business in 1884 at the lower end of Central Avenue. Four generations of the Loomis family were involved in several areas in the food business over the years. This plant was razed in 2005.

In 1906, the Loomis family interests purchased a small creamery, which was renamed Rosedale. Horses were used for home deliveries until the 1950s.

Rosedale started the production of ice cream in 1911 and became a pioneer in the production of ice-cream novelties. This is a 1940s photograph of women packing ice-cream bars.

The Fort Dodge Grocery Company, a major grocery wholesale house supplying grocery stores in a four-state area, was also a Loomis-affiliated business. It even handled its own name brand product line. Originally located on Central Avenue where the Wahkonsa Hotel is now, the company built this large headquarters and warehouse at 131 Central Avenue in the early 1900s.

The Loomis family owned Rosedale Farms on the east side of Fort Dodge and built the largest dairy barn in the county. In addition to cows, the family raised hogs, and one, Floyd of Rosedale, was given as settlement of a bet between the two governors on the Iowa-Minnesota football game. A sculpture of Floyd still serves as the traveling trophy in that football rivalry.

Before the introduction of mechanical refrigeration and production of ice at the time of World War I, all ice came from the Des Moines River. Harvesting the ice was done by hand and horses.

In 1910, three companies harvested 75,000 tons of ice from the river and stored it in large icehouses, such as the one shown here.

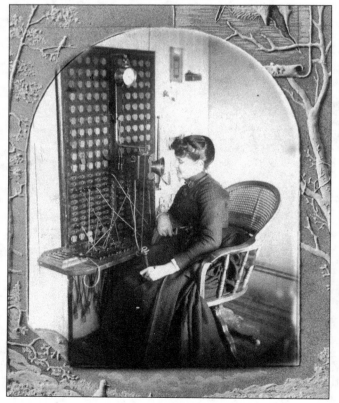

The telephone was invented in 1875, and it was only six years later that Fort Dodge had its first telephone exchange with a single "hello girl" and switchboard. By 1894, however, there were still only 52 telephones in the city. Four years later, there were 200, and by 1910, 3,300.

Five

STORES AND SERVICES

Today the size and location of Fort Dodge has made it a regional retail shopping and service center, but even in the early days, retail stores were the lifeblood of the community. The first retail business in Fort Dodge was the sutler's store operated by William Williams, and when the troops left, Williams continued to operate the store, serving the pioneer farmers. The earliest stores were all locally owned, and chain stores did not begin to have any impact until the 1920s. It has only been since the 1960s that the home-owned local proprietor has disappeared from the scene. Until the 1950s, almost all tradesmen, services, professional offices, and retail stores, with the exception of grocery stores, were concentrated in the downtown area. Unlike retail establishments, service institutions on a local level such as hospitals have been primarily a 20th-century development, and only since World War II have they served a regional constituency.

Fort Dodge Telephone Building.

The first telephone building was completed in 1912 and was located across the street from the Carnegie library.

In 1870, the Fort Dodge Gas and Coke Company was organized to provide illuminating gas for the city's streetlights, and in 1887, a plant was built to provide the city with its first electricity just eight years after Thomas Edison had invented his first lightbulb. It was in 1924 that the Fort Dodge Gas and Electric Company completed this building. All that remains is the lower dam, which provided water to run the steam turbines.

The oldest business in Fort Dodge is the Laufersweiler Funeral Home. In 2005, it was reported that it was the 82nd-oldest family-owned business in the nation. Conrad Laufersweiler came to Fort Dodge in 1858 as a furniture maker and soon added undertaking to his business pursuits. Until the 1920s, the funeral parlor and furniture business occupied the same building at 619 Central Avenue. The furniture business closed in 1930.

Another early business was Jacob Brown Groceries, located at 15 South Sixth Street. Opened in 1864 by Jacob Brown, a Civil War veteran, it continued to operate until 1962. The store was very diverse in its offerings as shown in the signs advertising hay, feed, and patent medicines.

This is the interior of Jacob Brown Groceries in the late 1800s. Notice the limited amount of merchandise and the potbellied stove. Until the 1950s, most grocery stores were small and every neighborhood also had at least one. In 1930, 80 grocers were listed in the city directory.

Mullen's Cash Grocery in 1912 was located at 622 Central Avenue and was an upscale version of Brown's. Notice it was a cash grocery. Most grocery stores at this time sold their products on credit subject to payment at the end of the month. Grocery stores, like Mullen's, were not self-service stores. The customer told the clerk what he or she wanted, and the clerk found it on the shelves.

During most of the city's history, grocery stores only carried groceries. Separate markets handled fruits and vegetables, and butcher shops provided meat. This photograph, dated 1927, is of the Lawson meat market located on Central Avenue.

By the 1880s, general stores had all but disappeared from the scene in Fort Dodge. They were replaced increasingly by specialty stores. In 1912, Berryhill's Store handled newspapers, books, office supplies, toys, and sporting goods. It also had a pool hall in the back. The manager was S. B. Philpot, the man holding the white paper, a leader in organizing the local National Guard unit.

It was common for most stores to be very small. Note the inventory and the three clerks in Rudesill's Shoe and Boot Store, 602 Central Avenue, in 1912. Often there was no back room for storage. Everything was out on the shelves.

By World War I, larger stores and even department stores began making their appearance. One of the longtime anchors of downtown was Gates Dry Goods. The company began operations in Fort Dodge in 1882 and acquired the Berryhill Building, seen on the right, in 1929. It soon expanded to take over the adjacent properties, 714–720 Central Avenue. The buildings still exist today but with a modern facade added in the 1950s. Gates Dry Goods closed in the early 1970s, and the property was acquired by MacGregor's Furniture.

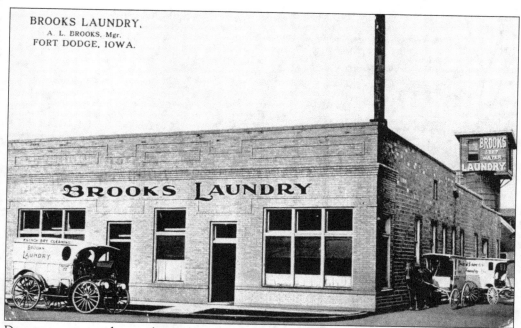

BROOKS LAUNDRY.
A. L. BROOKS. Mgr.
FORT DODGE. IOWA.

Downtown attracted not only retail establishments but also businesses providing services. Brooks Laundry, another long-term downtown business, opened its first shop at 15 North Eleventh Street about 1910.

There were several blacksmith shops downtown, this one being on First Avenue South. A blacksmith was often a jack-of-all-trades, frequently working on anything mechanical, in this case even automobiles.

Many businesses provided home delivery services. As indicated on the delivery truck, Atwell Florist provided special attention for parties, weddings, and funerals as early as 1912.

During the Great Depression of the 1930s, the Works Progress Administration built this city market at First Avenue South and Twelfth Street to provide market opportunities for small local food producers. Apparently it met with little success, and after World War II, the American Legion acquired the property for its clubhouse. The building burned in 1961.

Fort Dodge has had a reputation of being a wide-open town when it comes to vices. Saloons were a common part of local life. In 1908, the town sported 15. This early-20th-century Fort Dodge saloon is especially noteworthy in that it had a black bartender. Although Fort Dodge had African American residents dating to the earliest years, most would have worked only at a very menial labor level with little public contact.

Some establishments served several purposes. The Creole Inn, which opened in 1930 near the Illinois Central Railroad depot, served meals but was better known for its reputation as a brothel.

Fort Dodge was known for its restaurants. The Denver Café dates back to the early 1900s.

By 1930, the city directory listed 39 restaurants. Some started very small. The Dog House, located near what is now the Crossroads Mall, sold garden produce as well as hot dogs. Later a building housed it, and it was connected with the Sports Park automobile-racing track.

The most unique restaurant in Fort Dodge was the Kofy Pot Café on Twenty-second Street. It was opened in 1934 and appears to have closed about four years later. Outdoor seating was in booths shaped like coffee cups. Its specialty was goon legs, a type of shish kebab, and, unlike most restaurants, the Kofy Pot sold beer. Upstairs was a dance floor. The structure was remodeled into apartments, and in the 1970s, it was razed.

The most legendary of all the Fort Dodge restaurants was Treloar's. L. D. Treloar, who first came to Fort Dodge about 1920, ran a small hamburger place on Central Avenue and a sandwich wagon that traveled to county fairs.

By 1932, L. D. Treloar opened a makeshift restaurant at the north edge of town on Fifteenth Street and established a reputation for chicken and ribs.

The restaurant went through many changes and improvements over the years. In 1946, it had taken on this appearance.

In the 1950s, he opened the Country Boy Drive In, next to the Fifteenth Street restaurant, complete with carhops.

"Papa" Treloar also catered many community events at a time when most businesses and organizations had annual employee or member picnics.

By the 1960s, Treloar's had a statewide reputation and had become a destination restaurant. It burned in the 1970s and was never rebuilt.

The first hospital was not established until 1895 when a group of doctors and nurses acquired the residence located at First Avenue North and Sixth Street previously used by the Fort Dodge Presbyterian Collegiate Institute. It was furnished by local organizations and individuals who volunteered money and equipment. With Fort Dodge's growing population of about 12,000, the hospital with only 18 beds soon proved far too small.

St. Joseph Hospital, Fort Dodge, Io.

A typhoid epidemic in 1907 forced the community to reassess the health care system, and the Catholic order of the Sisters of Mercy offered to provide funds for a new hospital subject to a community dollar match. St. Joseph's Mercy Hospital, which was staffed and managed by the order, was dedicated in March 1909. The hospital also opened a school for nurses that had 560 graduates before it closed in 1959.

Immediately after World War I, the Lutheran denomination proposed the construction of a second hospital to be located on the west side of the river. Construction began in 1924, but financing failed and work ceased. It was not until 1930, assisted by a gift from O. M. Oleson, that construction resumed, and the building was dedicated in 1932. The two hospitals merged in the 1960s.

Most of the health care institutions were privately owned and for profit. Boulder Lodge Sanitarium was established in 1902 on the north edge of Fort Dodge by Dr. John Kime for the treatment of tuberculosis, a highly contagious and dreaded disease that in most cases was fatal.

Kime's treatment placed emphasis on rest, fresh air, and sunshine, and his patients lived in tents as long as weather permitted. After his death in 1911, the sanitarium's main building was purchased by Jett Wray, who operated it as a fashionable tearoom and restaurant in the 1930s and 1940s. Parts of the original building still exist and are incorporated into today's Wraywood Manor.

The Carver Eye, Ear, Nose and Throat Clinic was located at 1003 Central Avenue, the current site of the Carver building. The imposing Italianate-style home of Dr. Carver, one of the city's first medical specialists, was built around 1885 and was remodeled into a clinic in 1900. In 1918, the home was demolished and replaced with the Carver building.

The German Evangelical Lutheran Church organized the Kinderfreund Society in 1902 and opened the first orphanage in Fort Dodge in a house at 1819 Sixth Avenue North. Its bylaws called for the acceptance of neglected children who were not handicapped.

In 1930, the Kinderfreund Society, renamed the Lutheran Home Finding Society, moved into a new building in Round Prairie at 234 Ninth Avenue North.

Hope Hall was a social experiment instituted by Lorenzo Coffin, a reformer and philanthropist, arguably the most widely known person from Fort Dodge of his time. In the late 1890s, Coffin built it as a home for recently released convicts to facilitate a transition from prison life to life on the outside. Later the building was managed by the Women's Christian Temperance Union as a home for teenage unwed mothers. The structure, located a mile northwest of Fort Dodge on the Coffin farm, burned and the girls' home was moved to Des Moines.

Six

ETHNICS AND NEIGHBORHOODS

Fort Dodge was originally settled by people who moved in from the northeastern United States, generally several generations removed from Europe. After the Civil War, immigrants from Sweden, Norway, Germany, and Ireland began arriving in the area. By the start of the 20th century, Fort Dodge was benefitting from the general influx of immigration that the rest of the country was experiencing. By 1920, about 30 percent of the local population was of foreign birth. Identifiable ethnic groups included Germans, Swedes, Irish, Czechs, Slovaks, Italians, Mexicans, Greeks, Syrians, and Jews.

Fort Dodge historically has been divided into neighborhoods with interesting names such as Bob Town, the Flats, Pleasant Valley, Round Prairie, and Swede Town. Some neighborhoods were identified with specific ethnic groups: Swedes in West Fort Dodge, Italians in east Fort Dodge, Irish in the area around Corpus Christi Church. Other ethnic groups that lacked large numbers were less inclined to live in identifiable areas but still maintained close-knit social communities.

Swede Town, or West Fort Dodge, which was physically separated from the rest of Fort Dodge by the Des Moines River, maintained its ethnic identity until after World War II. This postcard, dated 1908, was taken from the Swede Town hill looking across the Des Moines River toward the main part of the city. The single bridge shown was the only connecting link with the rest of the city.

This photograph, taken looking east on Avenue C, catches the small-town flavor of neighborhood. About 90 percent of its population was Swedish, and the language was commonly used until well after World War I.

One of the first businesses on the west side was the Moe General Store, shown here and dating to the 1870s. The neighborhood was in some ways self-contained. In 1930, there were 15 retail and service businesses, including four grocery stores. It also had its own post office complete with its own postal cancellation.

The Paramount gas station was one of two stations located there. Note what appears to be a race car by the building on the right.

In the early 1900s, Riverside School was built on Avenue C. It replaced a wood frame school, which had served the Swedish population earlier.

The largest church on the west side was the Lutheran church at 300 J Street, shown in this photograph. In the late 1940s, the congregation voted to join Bethlehem Lutheran, a Swedish congregation that had a church at Eleventh Avenue and First Avenue North. The combined congregation became Grace Lutheran. The west side building now serves the Full Gospel Lighthouse Church, and the Bethlehem church has been remodeled into a private residence.

The second Swedish church on the west side was the Swedish Mission Church located at 1122 Avenue B. The church belongs to the Evangelical Covenant denomination, which has its origins in the southern part of the county in the 1870s. The local church was organized a few years later. The original building still stands, but the congregation, now First Covenant Church, has a new building near Highway 169.

Fort Dodge has had an African American presence dating back before the Civil War, but it is only since the 1950s that Fort Dodge has had an identifiable black neighborhood. The most prominent institution in the black community has been the church, and the oldest church is the Second Baptist. Established in 1886, the first building was located at 1827 Fourth Avenue South, the same location as the current church.

This is the Second Baptist ladies' group with Pastor Brooks in the 1950s.

The most widely recognized member of the black community in the post–World War II period was Harry Merryweather, who owned and operated Harry's Chicken Shack located beneath the Herring Viaduct. He was generally seen as the spokesman for the local African Americans. He is still honored with a scholarship fund in his name.

Rayford Johnson was, for obvious reasons, the most recognizable black person in Fort Dodge in the 1940s and 1950s. He was seven feet seven inches tall at a time when six feet six inches was tall, wore size 24 shoes, and played professional basketball for the Harlem Road Kings.

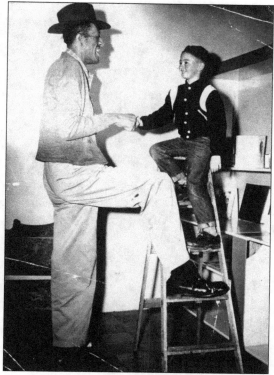

One of the longest-lasting businesses in Fort Dodge was the Chinese-owned Wing Lee Laundry, which was established in Fort Dodge about 1870. The business passed down through the family and continued until 1942 when the owners left to work in defense industries. Amazingly successful, the owners established other laundries in other Iowa communities. At the time of this photograph in the 1920s, the laundry was located at 1023 Central Avenue.

Members of the Italian community began arriving in Fort Dodge about 1910, attracted by jobs in the brick and tile plants. Once they were established, they moved first into grocery stores and later restaurants. One of the more successful grocery store families was the Cacioppos, who started this store in 1920. Other Italian grocers were Comamo, Segreto, Lorenzo, Mortillaro, Armato, and Amanzio.

Most of the local Jewish people arrived in Fort Dodge between 1905 and 1920, and in 1920, the Jewish population exceeded 200. Over the years, over 600 different individuals have at one time or another identified with the Jewish community. Many were merchants, and at one time, 7 of 15 local clothing stores were Jewish owned. In 1948, they built Beth El Synagogue.

Falling membership numbers led to the closure of the synagogue and its sale to the Presbyterian Church. The furnishings shown here were given to the Jewish Historical Center in Des Moines. The building is now the Shalom Center and used for youth community programs.

St. Olaf Lutheran is another church with strong ethnic origins. It was established originally as a mission church of the Norwegian church in Badger. The building is located on First Avenue South and Fourth Street. In the early 1950s, the congregation built a new church, and the old building is now Coppin Chapel, an African Methodist Episcopal church.

In the 1870s, Fort Dodge had a great influx of German immigrants, and their German heritage could be seen in their church, St. Paul Lutheran Church, and its German school. German-language services continued until World War I forced the congregation to turn to English. An addition to the church was built in 1930, but the church was destroyed by arson in 1999.

Slovak immigrants were attracted to Fort Dodge immediately after World War I. Working in the gypsum mills and the brickyards, they tended to concentrate in the southeast part of the city. Their SS. Peter and Paul Lutheran Church was constructed in 1929 at 1229 South Twenty-sixth Street. Today it is the home of Fort Dodge Pentecostal Ministries.

Seven

PARADES, PATRIOTISM, AND POLITICS

Parades, politics, and patriotism may be said to characterize community life in Fort Dodge during the first two decades of the 20th century. All three tended to bring the community together. This was a time in which the city was an extremely important political center in the state, as the home of two senators, three congressmen, the director of the U.S. Mint, the solicitor of the Department of the Treasury, and several other high-level national officials. Fort Dodge patriotism was reflected in a strong National Guard presence in the community, which brought local involvement in the national military adventures of the period. Parades were Fort Dodge's way of celebrating local events, honoring its heroes, and expressing local pride.

Fort Dodgers loved parades. Parades were held for the opening of the new school year, political events, the National Guard leaving for camp, the National Guard returning from camp, Memorial Day, the Fourth of July, lodge conventions, and whatever other excuse that might be found. The most glorious of the parades were the circus parades. Usually three or four circuses visited each summer, including the giant Barnum and Bailey. Circuses unloaded at the railroad yards and paraded down Central Avenue to the show grounds.

Political causes had their parades too. The largest political parade was the 1916 parade for women's suffrage and prohibition. Participants came from all over the state, and young ladies were recruited to pitch for the end of the liquor trade, not just in Iowa but in every land.

A strong moral cause did not always translate into good writing skills, as shown in this sign.

The other cause was women's suffrage. The women's right to vote was a vote for home and family. The surprising thing about this parade is that Fort Dodge, although in the 1870s there were some strong women advocates locally, was not a hotbed of either prohibition forces or the women's rights movement.

Parades for political causes continued over the years. In 1946, the local labor unions, a strong force in Fort Dodge at the time, faced with postwar inflation and general postwar economic adjustment problems and rallied to plead for a continuation of the Office of Price Administration and price controls.

In 1906, the Civil War veterans group the Grand Army of the Republic had its state convention here. The parade was led by an automobile followed by the National Association of Civil War Musicians band. Over 1,000 soldiers were said to have marched. The photograph was taken looking east from the city square.

All parades had their horses, their bands, and their kids.

The Women's Relief Corps, the auxiliary of the Grand Army of the Republic, had a presence in all patriotic parades through the 1930s.

In 1926, 20 years later, the Fort Dodge Memorial Day parade's special guests were a few Civil War veterans, still marching 60 years after the end of their war.

One expression of patriotism at the beginning of the 20th century was the establishment of a local National Guard unit. The first armory was located on the south side of the square. The National Guard was as much a social lodge as it was a military unit, sponsoring dances, carnivals, musical performances, and athletic events in order to raise funds needed but not provided by the government.

Associated with the local National Guard unit was the 56th Regimental Band, under the direction of Carl Quist. It might be considered the predecessor of the Fort Dodge Municipal Band, since it played for community events and dances. The band established a national reputation and traveled extensively.

In 1904, private funds built the armory at 710 First Avenue North, later the location of the Laramar Ballroom. It served the National Guard until 1951, when the armory was moved to the new municipal airport.

It was the source of great local pride, and in the next 25 years, the company was to serve during the Spanish-American War, on the Mexican border shortly before World War I, in World War I, and in several instances of governor call-up within the state.

World War I brought out great displays of patriotism. In July 1918, the local National Guard companies were called into service and marched down Central Avenue.

Floats constructed by citizen groups such as the Red Cross also participated in the parade to show their support. The Red Cross played a vital role during World War I within the community, and it gave the local women a sense of being an essential part of the war effort.

Thousands of Fort Dodgers turned out for the send-off. It was reported to have been the biggest community event in the city's history.

The National Guard companies departed from the Illinois Central Railroad depot. It was common for companies in the pre–World War I period to enter the service together and serve as a unit.

Draftees and new recruits were sent to Fort Des Moines and Camp Dodge for induction and basic training.

In the early part of the 20th century, the political reputation of Fort Dodge attracted many state and national leaders who made their presentations to the crowds in the city square.

In 1909, the governor of Iowa, Beryl Carroll, spoke in the city square. On the far right is Lorenzo Coffin, noted reformer, farmers' advocate, and humanitarian.

Pres. Theodore Roosevelt visited Fort Dodge in 1906 and made his trip down Central Avenue in a buggy.

Pres. William Taft visited Fort Dodge in 1911 and made a public presentation from the gazebo in the city square. Although other presidents and presidential candidates passed through the city on railroad whistle-stop campaigns, Taft was the last to spend any time here until Adlai Stevenson came to dedicate the airport in 1952, and John F. Kennedy stayed overnight in 1960.

Eight

THE GOOD LIFE

The quality of life in a community can be measured by the cultural, educational, and recreational opportunities that it provides, and Fort Dodge has from the very beginning offered a surprising variety. The soldiers hunted and fished, but they also arranged dances and put on dramatic and musical performances complete with costumes for their civilian neighbors. Land speculators pitched quotes for money but also had kept current through eastern and London newspapers delivered weekly by the stagecoach. Baseball was introduced by returning Civil War soldiers, and the National Guard played indoor baseball in its armory. Records indicate that one local resident, name unknown, had purchased a complete set of the published compositions of Bach in 1855. Maj. William Williams was a talented artist, Adeline Swain in the late 1860s was offering classes in painting to the young ladies in town, and David Gue, by 1870, had established a reputation in the East as a seascape and Hudson River valley landscape painter. By 1875, John F. Duncombe had established a zoo next to his home. With the arrival of the railroads, Fort Dodge opera houses hosted traveling lecturers and musical and theatrical groups.

In the 1920s, Fort Dodge Exposition Park was the home of the Hawkeye Exposition, a large regional fair with livestock exhibits, agricultural shows, and promotion of farm products. The park and fair lasted only through the 1920s, closing with the economic downturn of the 1930s.

The park was more than just a county fair grounds and had a permanent amusement park at which the featured ride was a roller coaster. The grounds also included such traditional rides as a carousel, wet water boats, a miniature railroad, bumper cars, a fun house, and carnival concessions. The city's only roller-skating rink occupied one of its buildings, and a gun club also made use of the grounds. For a few years, the Cardiff Giant, which was owned by local investors, was on display in one of the smaller buildings.

Some idea of the size of the park can be gotten from the size of the grandstand. Grandstand events included air shows and both horse and automobile racing featuring some of the nation's best. The most recognizable race car driver was the World War I flying ace Eddie Rickenbacker. The grandstand field also served as the first public golf course in the city. In the late 1930s, the grandstand, showing the effects of neglect and time, was demolished.

Managers of the park were innovative, often trying new things. Recognizing that the automobile was rapidly increasing in importance, a public campground was opened in 1922 just at a time that automobile camping was first beginning.

In 1925, a Bintz swimming pool was built on Exposition Park grounds. A highly innovative design, only one of about a dozen nationwide, it was entirely aboveground. Surprisingly the owners made the pool segregated. Only white kids were allowed. In 1936, when the Exposition Park Company went bankrupt, the city acquired the pool, and under the leadership of Ed Breen, the order was issued that discrimination would no longer be practiced. The pool was replaced by the present pool in the 1970s.

Other buildings on the grounds were livestock exhibition buildings, a large coliseum, and a pavilion. The pavilion, shown here, was transformed into the Expo Ballroom by Larry Geer, legendary ballroom owner and dance promoter, who also ran the Laramar downtown. The Expo Ballroom, which could be opened to the summer breezes, was used during the summer when the downtown ballroom became too warm. Like the Laramar, the Expo Ballroom attracted many nationally known big bands and large crowds.

During the 1920s through the 1950s, everyone danced. Most fraternal orders had weekly dances in their clubs, social organizations sponsored dances, and nightclubs featured live music. Small local bands thrived. Because of Fort Dodge's excellent train connections, virtually every big-name band in the nation at one time or another played there. In the 1940s and 1950s, teen dances became increasingly popular. The Laramar offered a teen night, but there were also the YMCA Blue Diamond dances and De Molay and Rainbow Girl formal dances. The dances featured live music and flourishing local bands.

The first golf course in Fort Dodge was laid out in 1899, just northwest of town. It had 81 members, and a golfer from Sioux City was hired to provide instruction. It failed, but over the years, other courses were established around town: private courses south of Swedetown, in southeast Fort Dodge near Oleson Park, a public course in Exposition Park in 1924, and today's Fort Dodge Country Club, shown here, which opened in 1912. In 1930, there were four golf courses in the community.

At the dawn of the 20th century, baseball was indeed America's favorite pastime. Local newspaper articles refer to it being played in Fort Dodge shortly after the Civil War. Shown here are the Tobin College team members of about 1910. Their competition was anyone willing to play them. The National Guard, the YMCA, and the high school also fielded teams, and a form of baseball was even played indoors.

Most of the local interest, however, was in a professional team that existed in Fort Dodge from about 1900 to World War I and often played against teams that barnstormed around the country. During that period, the Fort Dodge team was part of an Iowa baseball league, which included teams from many of the larger cities in Iowa. The Fort Dodge team had three men who later played in the major leagues.

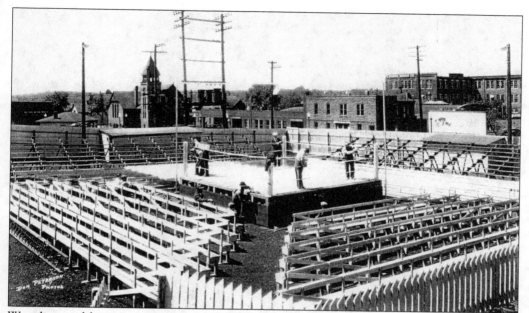

Wrestling and boxing enjoyed great popularity in Fort Dodge in the first decade of the 20th century, largely because of Frank Gotch, a world champion from Humboldt. In 1935, the ring, located on the south side of the square, featured both professional and semiprofessional boxing and wrestling.

After World War II, interest in boxing was renewed, primarily with the amateur Golden Gloves fights.

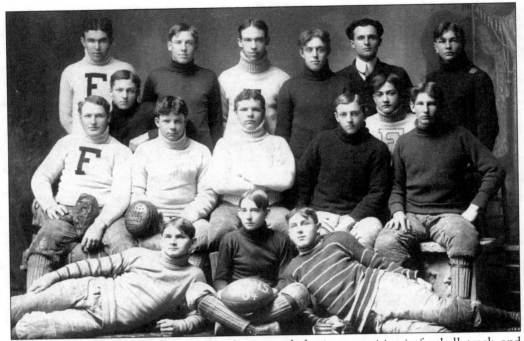

Fort Dodge High School became involved in interscholastic competition in football, track, and basketball, even before 1900. Here the 1904 football team poses for what may be the school's first official team photograph.

By 1940, the high school team had moved into the new Dodger Stadium. Its construction was a Works Progress Administration project, and the bricks used were recycled when the building that had been the old junior high school was razed. After the war, Fort Dodge High School was seen as one of the state's football powerhouses.

While Fort Dodge was proud of its competitive boys' sports, girls were limited to exercises and intramural sports. This photograph was taken in the gymnasium of the new high school in 1923.

Between 1870 and the 1920s, many theaters served Fort Dodgers and had been visited by hundreds of theatrical companies and entertainers who traveled the country. In many cases, the nation's best traveling by rail found Fort Dodge a convenient stop between major theatrical venues. By 1910, it was not unusual for three theaters to feature live entertainment on the same night. Shown here is the first large theater, the Midland, on the northwest corner of Ninth Avenue and First Avenue South. It opened in 1896 and seated over 900. It burned in 1908.

In 1910, the Princess Theatre, seating 900, was built as a vaudeville house, although later it featured motion pictures as well. It had its own house orchestra, and it attracted some of the biggest names in entertainment. The Depression and motion pictures killed many of the traveling shows, and the Princess Theatre closed in 1934. The building at 18 North Ninth Street became the First National Bank in 1939 and was razed in the 1970s to make room for the Wells Fargo Center.

Theatrical companies were frequently regional, traveling a set circuit. The Princess Theatre was home base for one of these groups in the 1920s, the Neale Helvey Players.

Movie theaters first appeared about 1905 and achieved great popularity quickly. The Magic Theater in 1908 reported offering three showings on a Saturday night with a total attendance of 1,000 and turning 200 away. In 1924, total seating capacity for the four movie theaters was 2,120. One of the most popular was the Rialto, 604 Central Avenue, which opened around 1920 and closed in 1973.

In the 1950s, local businesses provided free Saturday matinees for kids during the Christmas season. This shot of a Rialto Saturday matinee shows the size, 800 seats, and the odd seating arrangement.

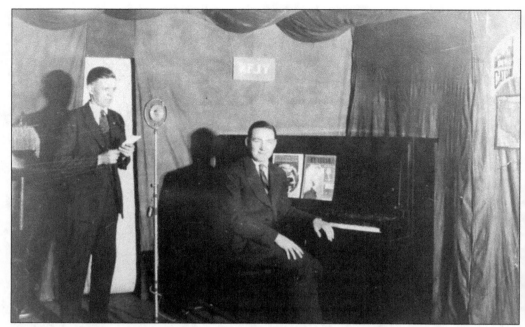

The first local radio station, KFJY, began broadcasting in the early 1920s, but the lack of many receivers made the venture unprofitable. It was not until Ed Breen's KVFD began broadcasting on Christmas Eve 1939 that the area had a successful station. With a strong emphasis on live broadcasting, including musical performances at the station, it was immediately successful. One of the most popular of the local programs featured Mary Varguson, on the piano, who played at many clubs and restaurants.

One of the station's most famous broadcasters was Gene Elston (right), shown here shortly after the war. Although he handled general broadcasting, his big interest was in sports. Elston went on in sportscasting to become the voice of the Houston Astros.

In October 1953, KQTV, later renamed KVFD-TV, began broadcasting television programs to an area with a 45-mile radius around Fort Dodge. Like the radio station, focus was placed on local programming.

One of the most popular programs was *Eve's Kitchen*, with Eve Rubenstein, featuring cooking demonstrations and women's interests. Her featured daily food creation was delivered to the home of a lucky winner. Rubenstein was recognized nationally as one of the pioneer women in television broadcasting and is in the Iowa Women's Hall of Fame.

Another popular show on KQTV was *Saturday Night Barn Dance*, sponsored by the Schultz Brothers automobile dealership. It featured the talents of local performers, sometimes with far more emphasis on local than on talent. Other programs included a live kids' program with "Aunt" Janet Wiewel and "Uncle" Dick Johnson and *Quiz Bowl* for students from the small towns in the surrounding area. The station went off the air in 1977 when a tornado damaged the tower and studio.

Fort Dodge has had a strong musical heritage, especially in band music. Although there were many bands in the 19th century, one of the most prominent was the Concordia Band. The Concordia Band was especially unique because it grew out of the members' association with the German Lutheran Church.

A second early band was the Fort Dodge Band. Most of these early bands were essentially all-purpose bands, performing in concerts and playing for dances and participating in the many parades that marched down Central Avenue. Some musicians played in several bands.

Karl King (1891–1971) was born in Ohio and at an early age joined the circus to play in its band. He went on to become one of the nation's leading composers of band music, best known for his "Barnum and Bailey's Finest" march. In 1920, he answered an advertisement for a position as director of the Fort Dodge Municipal Band, a position he held for the next 50 years. Through King's efforts, legislation was passed that gave municipalities the power to levy a tax for the support of a community band, and the Fort Dodge band was placed on a sound financial footing.

King established the reputation of the band as one of the nation's finest. Not only did it play local concerts, but it also became the official band for the Iowa State Fair and frequently traveled around the United States. This photograph is from 1931.

In 1938, the Oleson Park Band Pavilion, a Works Progress Administration project, was completed. Designed by the nationally recognized architect Henry Kamphoefner, it was chosen by the State of Iowa for its architectural excellence to be shown at the 1939 New York World's Fair. It is on the National Register of Historic Places.

In the 1920s, the Fort Dodge American Legion post organized a drum and bugle corps that achieved great success. In 1928, it won the American Legion national championship competition and traveled to Paris to participate in the 10th anniversary celebration of the World War I armistice.

Fort Dodge also has had a strong choral tradition. In the 1890s, a group of young Norwegian men, who gathered for social activities, cards, and singing, were organized by O. M. Oleson into the Fort Dodge Grieg Manskor to perpetuate Norwegian choral music. It was named after the great Norwegian composer Edvard Grieg. The *manskor* continued to perform until the 1960s. Oleson was knighted by the king of Norway for his contributions to Norwegian music.

In 1930, the Fort Dodge Men's Civic Glee Club was organized. By the year of this photograph, 1941, the choir had established a reputation and given performances around the state. In 1949, it performed in the first Men's Civic Glee Club Varieties, which for years was one of the musical highlights in the community. In recent years, women became an integral part of the organization, and its name was changed to the Fort Dodge Civic Glee Club.

From 1946 to 1959, the Harvest Festival was a major August celebration held in Dodger Stadium. Sponsored by local businesses, free tickets were given to people in surrounding communities as a thank-you for their patronage. The shows attracted thousands of spectators and followed a vaudeville-type format ranging from acrobats to musical performances.

At a time before kids' sports were highly organized, other games and activities kept them busy. The YWCA sponsored a citywide marbles tournament, and one local winner went on to win the national championship.

Returning veterans of World War II were eager to reestablish family life, and the postwar period was characterized by a focus on programs aimed at young people. One of the highlights was kids' fish day sponsored by the Izaac Walton League. At first it was held at a pond north of town along the Des Moines River but later was moved to the pond at Armstrong Park.

One of the highlights of the end of the year in Fort Dodge between 1930 and 1970 was the presentation of George Frideric Handel's *Messiah* by local musicians in the Fort Dodge High School auditorium. Always a sellout crowd, as shown in this photograph from 1947, it brought the community together. Today when many Americans are concerned with the quality of life and the loss of identity, a photographic history of a community can provide a sense of place and pride, which many find lacking. Hopefully this work can contribute to that end.

Visit us at
arcadiapublishing.com